world tour

Brazil

ADRIANA DOMINGUEZ

www.raintreepublishers.co.uk
Visit our website to find out more information about Raintree books.

To order:
- ☎ Phone 44 (0) 1865 888112
- 🖷 Send a fax to 44 (0) 1865 314091
- 🖳 Visit the Raintree Bookshop at **www.raintreepublishers.co.uk** to browse our catalogue and order online.

First published in Great Britain by Raintree Publishers, Halley Court, Jordan Hill, Oxford, OX2 8EJ, part of Harcourt Education.
Raintree is a registered trademark of Harcourt Education Ltd.

© Harcourt Education Ltd 2003
First published in paperback 2004
The moral right of the proprieter has been asserted.

Editorial: Sally Knowles
Cover Design: Peter Bailey and Michelle Lisseter
Production: Jonathan Smith

Printed and bound in China and Hong Kong by South China Printing Company

ISBN 1 844 21307 2 (hardback)
07 06 05 04 03
10 9 8 7 6 5 4 3 2 1

ISBN 1 844 21321 8 (paperback)
08 07 06 05 04
10 9 8 7 6 5 4 3 2 1

British Library Cataloguing in Publication Data
Dominguez, Adriana
Brazil (World tour)
981
A full catalogue for this book is available from the British Library

Acknowledgements
The publishers would like to thank the following for permission to reproduce photographs: p.**1a** © Jacues Jangoux; p.**1b** © Stephanie Maze/CORBIS; p.**1c** © Staffan Widstrand/ CORBIS; p.**3a** © Reuters NewMedia Inc/CORBIS; p.**3b** ©Jacues Jangoux; p.**5** ©Karl Kummels/SuperStock; p.**6** ©Nik Wheeler/CORBIS; p.**7** ©Jonathan Blair/CORBIS; p.**8** ©Karl Kummels/ SuperStock; p.**13** ©Jacues Jangoux; p.**14** ©Jeremy Horner/ CORBIS; p.**16** ©Haroldo de Faria Castro/Getty Images; p.**19** ©Dave G. Houser/ Houserstock; p.**21a** ©Owen Franken/ CORBIS; p.**21b** ©Tom Brakefield/CORBIS; p.**23** ©Rogerio Reis/Latin Focus; p.**25a** ©John Langford; p.**25b** ©Joe McDonald/CORBIS; pp.**27,28** ©Stephanie Maze/CORBIS; p.**29** ©J.R. Couto/Latin Focus; p.**31a** ©Julian Calder/CORBIS; p.**31b** © Marcelo Soubhia/Latin Focus; pp.**34,35** ©Steven Mark Needham/ FoodPix/Getty Images; p.**37a** ©Staffan Widstrand/CORBIS; p.**37b** ©Victor Englebert/Photo Researchers, Inc.; p.**38a** ©Jacues Jangoux/Getty Images; p.**40** ©Stephanie Maze/CORBIS; p.**43b** ©Jacues Jangoux; pp.**44a, 44b** ©TimePix; p.**44c** ©Moshe Shai/CORBIS.

Additional Photography by Comstock Royalty Free, PhotoDisc, and the Steck-Vaughn Collection.

Cover photography: Background: Getty Images/Imagebank/Anthony Boccaccio. Foreground: Corbis/Stephanie Maze.

Contents

Welcome to Brazil

Brazil is the largest country in South America and it is a wonderful place to visit. It has famous carnival celebrations and it is home to the Amazon Rainforest, one of the most mysterious and beautiful rainforests in the world. There are tall mountains, sandy beaches and exciting cities.

Reader's tips

• Use the table of contents

Do you already know what you are looking for? Maybe you just want to know what topics this book will cover. The contents page tells you what topics you will read about. It tells you where to find them in the book.

• Look at the pictures

This book has lots of great photos. Flip through and look at the pictures you like best. This is a great way to get a quick idea of what this book is all about. Read the captions to learn more about the photos.

• Use the index

If you are looking for a certain fact, then you might want to turn to the index at the back of the book. The index lists the subjects covered in the book. It will tell you what pages to find them on.

▲ **BRASILIA**
Brasilia is not the biggest city in Brazil, but it is the capital.
This modern city is home to Brazil's government.

Brazil's past

Brazil has a fascinating history and learning about the country's past is a good way to understand modern Brazil and the people who live there.

Early history

Very little is known about the **Native** Americans who lived in Brazil before the Europeans discovered it. We do know that most of them were Tupí-Guaraní. The Tupí-Guaraní lived off their small crop farms. There were between 2 and 5 million Native Americans living in Brazil when Europeans arrived.

Discovery by the Portuguese

In 1500, an explorer called Pedro Álvares Cabral sailed from Lisbon in Portugal to find a **trade route** to India. Instead, he found Brazil. King João III of Portugal sent the first settlers there in 1531.

These settlers were Portuguese criminals. They lived with the native Tupís and learnt to speak their language. The natives taught them how to farm and hunt. Some settlers and natives married each other.

◄ **PORTUGUESE KNIGHTS**
Native Tupí Indians were no match for Portuguese soldiers wearing armour and riding horses.

6

CHOPPING SUGAR CANE ▶
The Portuguese quickly learnt that sugar cane grows well in Brazil. Natives and African slaves were the first sugar cane workers.

The settlers noticed that Brazil was a perfect place for growing sugar cane. Sugar is made from sugar cane. For most of the 1500s, the native Tupís worked as slaves on the sugar **plantations**. Many slaves died from hard labour and European diseases. In the 1600s, the Portuguese brought African slaves to Brazil to replace the Native Americans. Marriages between Europeans, Tupís and Africans are one reason that modern Brazil is made up of so many different **cultures**.

In 1807, the French emperor Napoleon conquered Portugal and the Portuguese royal family escaped to Brazil. King João VI returned to Portugal after Napoleon left in 1821. His son Pedro stayed in Brazil. In 1822, Pedro was crowned Emperor of Brazil.

▲ **BRASILIA'S TOWERS**
The Brazilian congress meets in these tall buildings.

The 'Old Republic'

In the 1800s, coffee became more important than sugar cane. The owners of coffee plantations became very rich and wanted slavery to continue. They were very unhappy when the emperor **abolished** slavery in 1888, and looked for someone else to control the country.

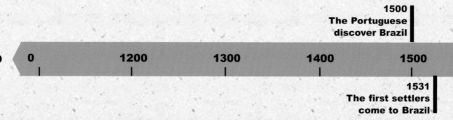

1500
The Portuguese
discover Brazil

AD 0   1200   1300   1400   1500

1531
The first settlers
come to Brazil

In 1889, General Manuel Deodoro da Fonseca led a **revolt** to overthrow the Brazilian emperor and declared Brazil a **republic**. He was then elected its first president.

Brazil today

The 20th century was very difficult for Brazil. The government was not always **democratic**. The 'Second Republic' was created in 1945 and lasted until the military took control of Brazil in 1964. Brazil became a democracy again in 1985. Brazil's first capital was Salvador, on the eastern coast, but it was moved to Brasilia in 1960.

Many of Brazil's problems continue. Brazil owes lots of money to other countries. Many people in Brazil are very poor while others are very rich. Not everyone agrees with the government's plans to help the country, but many people think that things have improved since democracy was restored.

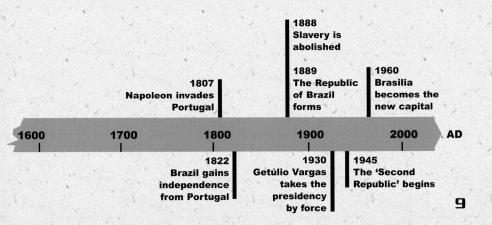

1888 Slavery is abolished

1889 The Republic of Brazil forms

1960 Brasilia becomes the new capital

1807 Napoleon invades Portugal

1600   1700   1800   1900   2000   AD

1822 Brazil gains independence from Portugal

1930 Getúlio Vargas takes the presidency by force

1945 The 'Second Republic' begins

A look at Brazil's geography

Brazil's forests are very famous. The Portuguese named the land after its beautiful brasilwood trees which are still found in the Amazon rainforest. The Amazon rainforest makes up 30 per cent of all the rainforests in the entire world. Many people visit Brazil to go on **ecological** tours of the rainforest. Ecological tours teach people about the important animals and plants that live in a particular place.

Land

Most of Brazil's land is low-lying and flat. It is almost impossible to think of Brazil without thinking of the Amazon rainforest. A rainforest is a place where trees and plants grow tall and close together and the air is warm and humid. Rainforest covers almost half of Brazil. It stretches 6,000,000 square kilometres (2,300,000 square miles) from the north to western and central Brazil.

There are several mountain ranges along the Atlantic coast. The tallest mountain, called Pico de Neblina, is 3014 metres tall. The mountains in Brazil are not the tallest in the world but the Brazilian mountains that rise next to the ocean are incredibly beautiful.

BRAZIL'S SIZE ▶
Brazil is the fifth-largest country in the world and the largest country in South America. It covers 8,511,965 sq km (3,286,474 sq miles). Brazil is so large that it borders every country in South America except Chile and Ecuador.

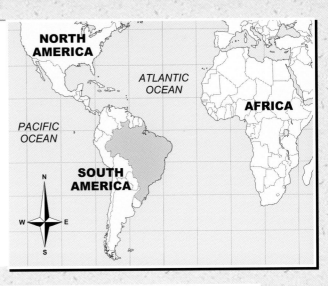

BRAZIL

★ National capital
● Major citiy
— River

0 200 400 Kilometres
0   200   400 Miles

Water

Brazil has the largest river in the world, the Amazon. It is not as long as the Nile in Africa, but it holds much more water. The Amazon is in the northern part of the country and flows east to the Atlantic Ocean passing right through the Amazon rainforest. The Amazon and the rivers that connect to it provide water for most of the plants and animals that live in the rainforest.

Another amazing site in Brazil is the Iguaçu Falls. The falls lie along the Argentina-Paraguay border in the south. They are nearly 3 kilometres (2 miles) wide, and average 71 m high.

Brazil is also known for its beautiful beaches, and there are plenty of them – the country's coastline is 7491 kilometres (4654 miles) long. Much of Brazil lies on the **equator**, so the sun is very strong.

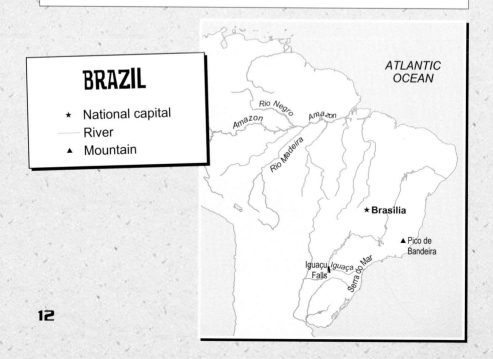

BRAZIL

★ National capital
— River
▲ Mountain

▲ THE MIGHTY AMAZON
The great river Amazon winds through Brazil. It is surrounded by lush, green rainforest.

Climate

Brazil's climate is very warm and most of the country does not get cold even in winter. Although it is hot, there is often heavy rain. The region around the Amazon rainforest is close to the equator. The average temperature there is about 27°C. Rainforests are also very **humid** and get far more rain than anywhere else, which is how they get their name.

Brazil is on the opposite side of the equator to Europe and the USA, and on the same side as Australia. Europe and the USA are in the northern half of the globe, above the equator. Brazil and Australia are in the southern half of the globe. When it is winter in London and New York, it is summer in Brazil and Sydney.

▲ **THE RAINFOREST**
Thick clouds pour rain on one part of the rainforest.

Rio de Janeiro: snapshot of a big city

▲ RIO'S COASTLINE
Mountains rise over São Conrado Beach, where Rio de Janeiro meets the Atlantic Ocean.

Rio, as it is commonly known, is the second-largest city in Brazil. More than 6 million people live there. Rio is also Brazil's best-known city.

City facts

Rio de Janeiro is on a **bay** on the Atlantic Ocean. Portuguese explorers named it when they arrived in 1502. They thought they had found the mouth of a river. Rio de Janeiro means 'River of January' in Portuguese. Later, the city's official name became São Sebastião do Rio de Janeiro but nobody calls it by that name because it is too long.

Rio is Brazil's most important **port**. Its harbour is one of the largest in the world. The people of Rio produce much of Brazil's food, clothing and chemicals.

Rio is also famous for its beaches and scenery. At the entrance to the bay, there is a tall, pointed mountain called Pão de Açúcar (Sugar Loaf Mountain). Corcovado Mountain stands near it and together they are an amazing sight.

Main attractions

The best way to see Rio's beaches is to walk along Avenida Atlántica. Make sure you visit Copacabana Beach, the most famous beach in Rio.

You can climb Sugar Loaf Mountain or Corcovado Mountain for great views of the city. One of the most famous sights is the statue of Jesus on the top of Corcovado. It is easy to see from the ground.

The statue is called Cristo Redentor (Christ the Redeemer). It stands 701 metres above **sea level** and is 29.5 metres tall, excluding the pedestal. It weighs 1,163,377 kilograms. A 20-minute train ride from Cosme Velho will take you to the top of the mountain.

A historical tour

Quinta da Boã Vista is Rio's largest historic park. It was built in the 1600s and given as a gift to the Portuguese royal family. Like most parks, it has beautiful gardens and lawns but it also has lakes, caves and islands. There is also a zoo and many museums, including the National Museum. The National Museum has exhibits that tell you about Brazil's history, plants, animals and minerals.

Praça Quinze is a square surrounded by 12 historic buildings and it is an ideal place to learn about Brazilian history. There are lots of churches in Rio. This is because the Portuguese brought the Roman Catholic religion to Brazil and it became very popular. Now most Brazilians are Catholic.

More things to do

The Teatro Paço Imperial is well worth a visit. It was built in the 1700s. It was originally built as a palace for the emperor but it is now an important theatre. For people who are more interested in sports, Maracaná Stadium is ideal. It is Brazil's most famous football stadium and one of the largest in the world – it can hold 100,000 people.

COPACABANA BEACH ▶
This vendor is selling wide-brimmed hats on Copacabana Beach. A hat offers good protection from the strong Brazilian sun.

RIO DE JANEIRO'S TOP-TEN CHECKLIST

Here is a list of the top ten things you should do if you go to Rio.

- ☐ Walk in the busy area around Copacabana Beach.
- ☐ Take a cable car to the top of Sugar Loaf Mountain.
- ☐ See the 4536 kg meteorite on display at the National Museum.
- ☐ Visit the zoo in Quinta Da Boã Vista.
- ☐ Have a look at the Brazilian landmarks around Praça Quinze.
- ☐ Listen to street musicians and have a picnic in Largo do Boticário.
- ☐ See the ruins of old mansions in Parque das Ruinas in Santa Teresa.
- ☐ Spend some time at Nossa Senhora da Glória do Outeiro church.
- ☐ See a play or have dinner at the Teatro Paço Imperial.
- ☐ Go to Maracaná Stadium and watch a football game.

Four top sights

Brazil is a very large country. Even people who live there have not seen it all. Here are some suggestions to help you experience the best of what Brazil has to offer.

The river Amazon

People called *caboclos* live in the towns along the banks of the river Amazon. The *caboclos* live off the **natural resources** of the rainforest.

Hundreds of types of animal live in the rainforest. Many of them, like tapirs and monkeys, go to the Amazon to drink its water or to catch **prey**. There are rare dolphins called tucuxi dolphin living there. They are one of the smallest species of dolphin in the world, and are unusual because dolphins do not usually live in rivers. There are electric eels and piranha fish in the Amazon. Be careful – piranhas like to eat fresh meat and electric eels can give you a severe electric shock.

Many different **species** of colourful bird live in the trees including toucans, parrots and hummingbirds. Lots of insects live around the river. There are more than 1800 species of butterfly and more than 200 species of mosquito in the rainforest. Insect repellent and a mosquito net are useful to avoid being bitten.

All these animals, and a lot of people, depend on the Amazon for their survival. The Amazon is not just a river – it is an important source of life.

▼ LIFE ON THE AMAZON

A young boy rows a dugout canoe through thick jungle. Many Native Americans still live along the river Amazon.

TAPIR CALF ▶

A baby tapir is born with stripes and spots. This pattern helps to hide it from enemies. The patterns will disappear as the calf gets older.

Salvador da Bahia

Salvador da Bahia is a city packed with historic buildings and amazing beaches. It sits between green **tropical** hills and the bay of Todos os Santos. The city was built on two levels. Houses and other buildings were built on the hills while the forts, docks and warehouses were built on the beaches. Electric lifts, called Elevador Lacerda, carry more than 50,000 passengers from one level of the city to the other every day. They travel 71 metres in less than 15 seconds.

Salvador was founded in 1549 and remained Brazil's most important city for more than 200 years. It was famous for its beautiful mansions and churches decorated with gold. The city has 34 **colonial** churches

It is easy to see the influence of African culture on Brazilian life during the Carnival festival each year. Tourists from all over the world travel to see the Carnival festivals. There are parades with music and dancing, as well as special food – all displaying a mixture of African and Brazilian culture. If you cannot go to Carnival, you can still learn about Brazilian African culture at Salvador's Museu Afro-Brasileira. It tells the story of Brazil's links with Africa and how the two cultures have combined.

▲ **ELEVADOR LACERDA IN SALVADOR**
Travel by Elevador Lacerda in Salvador da Bahia.
It will take you from the bottom of the city to the top in
less than 15 seconds.

Iguaçu Falls

The Iguaçu Falls are some of the most beautiful waterfalls in the world. The name Iguaçu comes from a Native American word meaning 'great water'. The water for these falls flows from the river Iguaçu and runs through the Serra do Mar mountains. It makes its way west for 1320 kilometres (820 miles) and widens around the Brazilian jungle. At the border of Argentina and Paraguay, the river crashes down to form the huge Iguaçu Falls.

Iguaçu Falls are made up of 275 different waterfalls, or cataracts. It is a breathtaking sight. There are also some spectacular trees and other plants that grow nearby. There are colourful orchids growing next to pines and bamboo sprouting alongside palm trees. It is unusual to see these types of plants growing right next to each other. Many interesting animals make their homes in this area, including jaguars, monkeys and deer.

Visiting the Falls is thrilling as you can feel the power of the water. You will hear their thunder and feel the spray. There are catwalks, which are narrow walkways with guardrails. You can walk along a catwalk and look over the falls. Sometimes floods block the way to the catwalks. The best time of year to go to the Iguaçu Falls is between August and November, when the risk of flooding is small.

▲ **THE WATERFALLS**
Visitors make their way carefully along catwalks near the falls. Guardrails stop people from falling in.

◀ **SPINY LITTLE DEVIL**
This spiny devil katydid lives near Iguaçu Falls. Katydids take up this pose to threaten predators. Their green colour helps to hide them in the trees, but they can move quickly if they are in danger.

Carnival in Rio

Brazilians say that their Carnival is the biggest celebration in the world and they are probably right. Rio de Janeiro's Carnival is famous throughout the world. Many people visit Rio in February just to see it because the entire city turns into a huge party parade.

Carnival is a five-day festival that ends on Shrove Tuesday and marks the beginning of Lent. African culture and rhythms heavily influence Brazil's Carnival and its music.

During Carnival, there is music, dancing and people dressed in amazing costumes everywhere. Many Cariocas people (as the people of Rio are called) spend a lot of time and money to prepare the floats, costumes and dances for the celebration. Some take a whole year to prepare. These are the people who compete in Carnival's best-known event, called the **Samba** School Parade. A samba school is not a school for children. It is a group of people who get together to celebrate Carnival. A single school may have up to 5000 people.

During the Samba School Parade, schools compete with each other in front of a **jury**. Each samba school must have a theme. Sometimes, the theme is an historical event or person. Other times, it is a Brazilian story or legend. The costumes must reflect the theme's historical time and place. The samba song must tell a story, and the floats must do a good job of showing the theme if that samba school is to win the grand prize.

▲ **A PARTY TO REMEMBER**
Carnival is one of the greatest parties in the world. This amazing five-day festival dazzles visitors with floats, samba dancers, Afro-Brazilian music and much more.

Going to school in Brazil

Children in Brazil go to school between the ages of seven and fourteen. When they are fourteen, many children leave school to help at home or find work. Others stay in high school and may go on to college.

Brazilian schools are very similar to schools in England, Australia and the USA. Students study subjects like maths, science and history. Classes in Brazil are taught in Portuguese, the national language. There are many international schools in Brazil. International schools often teach classes in a language other than Portuguese, such as English or German. There are also religious schools. Most religious schools are Catholic.

▲ AT SCHOOL IN BRAZIL...
These children study many of the subjects that you do.
Classes are taught in Portuguese, the national language.

Brazilian sports

In Brazil, football is called *futebol*. The national team is one of the best in the world and has won the highest football prize, the World Cup, five times. Brazilians are very proud of their team. They like to play football almost as much as they like to talk about it.

Brazilians play many other sports, too. Motor racing, horse racing, tennis, volleyball and water polo are all very popular there. Brazilians also like to play a game called *boliche*, which is like bowls. In boliche, players use several heavy black or brown balls which they roll across the ground.

▲ FOOTBALL STADIUM
Football is one of the country's favourite sports. If you can play it, or even talk about it, you will make friends immediately.

From farming to factories

When the Portuguese first came to Brazil, they noticed that the land and climate were perfect for growing sugar cane. Later, they grew coffee too. Many discovered that they could make more money from coffee than from sugar. Brazil's land is still very rich today, and farming is still important. Farmed products, including coffee, bring in a lot of money to Brazil's **economy**. The kind of money people use in Brazil is called the **reàl** (RAY-al).

The Amazon rainforest is very important to the country's economy. Trees are used for **timber**. The land is used to raise cattle, among other things. Many people in Brazil and all over the world are trying to stop the destruction of the rainforest, but beef and timber are important to Brazil's economy, so this is not easy to do.

Like the rest of the world, Brazil is becoming more modern. Today, fewer Brazilians are farmers. More people work in factories. Brazilian factories make **textiles**, shoes, chemicals, aeroplanes, cars and car parts. These export products are sold to other countries.

There are many poor people in Brazil. In Brazil, the poor people are very poor and the rich are very rich. The government is trying to help its poor people live better lives.

COFFEE BEANS ▶

The beans are dried and specially prepared. They are then ground and brewed into coffee.

▼ **A CAR FACTORY**

Brazilian workers on an assembly line put the finishing touches to new cars. Many cars will be exported – sent to other countries for sale.

The Brazilian government

Brazil is a republic. In a republic, the people vote for members of the government. Brazil's government is made up of three different parts, or branches. These three parts are called the executive, legislative and judicial branches.

The executive branch is made up of the president, vice president and the cabinet. The president and vice president are elected by the people and serve for four years. The cabinet is a group of people the president chooses to help him or her. The executive branch makes sure that laws are obeyed.

The legislative branch is the National Congress, which makes the laws. It is made up of the Federal Senate and the Chamber of Deputies. The judicial branch is made up of judges. They make sure that the laws are fair.

BRAZIL'S NATIONAL FLAG

The flag of Brazil has a green background with a large yellow diamond in the centre. In the middle of the diamond is a blue circle. It has 27 stars and a banner. On the banner is written 'Ordem e Progresso', which means 'Order and Progress'. The green stands for the fields and forests of Brazil. The yellow diamond represents its gold supply. The blue circle and stars represent the night sky over Brazil's capital and its 26 states.

Religions of Brazil

About 80 per cent of Brazilians are Roman Catholic. Catholics practise a form of the Christian religion. Christians follow the teachings of Jesus as written in the New Testament of the Bible. Today, nearly every town in Brazil has a church. Roman Catholics follow a religious leader called the pope.

The number of Protestants in Brazil has also grown. Protestantism is now the second most important religion in the country. Protestantism is another form of Christianity but Protestants do not follow the pope.

Other religious groups, such as Jews and Buddhists, make up 3 to 5 per cent of Brazil's population. Candomblé is a religion that was created by African slaves. It mixes African and Christian beliefs. In recent years, it has become more popular.

BRAZIL'S CHURCHES ▶
European colonists founded many of Brazil's oldest Catholic churches. These historic churches are still in use today.

Brazilian food

There is very little fast food in Brazil. Brazilians like to take the time to sit back and enjoy their meals. Breakfast is the only small and quick meal they eat. A typical Brazilian breakfast is coffee or milk, bread and jam, fresh fruit and sometimes cheese and ham.

Lunch and dinner are times to sit down, relax and talk with family and friends. Dinner is usually eaten very late at night. The meals are large and there is often a lot to choose from.

Beef is an important food in Brazil and barbecues are very popular. The national dish of Brazil is called *feijoada*. It is Brazilian black beans in a stew, with lots of beef and sausage. Rice, corn, tomatoes and sweet peppers are also used a lot in Brazilian cooking.

Desserts in Brazil are often based on the wonderful fruits that are grown here, like mangoes, guavas and papayas. Often these fruits are made into excellent ice cream. There is also a pudding called *Pudim de Leite*, the delicious Brazilian custard flan.

◀ FEIJOADA
Brazilian-style black beans are a favourite choice in homes and restaurants.

Brazil's recipe

PUDIM DE LEITE

INGREDIENTS:
200 g sugar (for the caramel)
1 tin sweetened condensed milk
Equal amount of ordinary milk
(use the condensed milk tin to measure)
3 eggs
20-cm circular mould
Roasting tin

WARNING:
**Never cook or bake by yourself.
Always ask an adult to help you
in the kitchen.**

DIRECTIONS:
**Place 2.5 to 5 cm of water in a roasting tin. Ask an adult to
help you put the tin in the oven and preheat to 160° C or
gas mark 2. Put the sugar in the mould. Ask an adult to help
you put the mould on the cooker, over medium heat and to
help you to keep turning the mould until the sugar melts into
a golden brown caramel. Be careful not to burn the sugar or
yourself (use oven gloves to hold the mould). Pour the
caramel into another dish. Let the mould cool. Combine the
condensed milk, ordinary milk and eggs in a blender, and
whip until smooth. Pour this mixture into the mould and place
it in the centre of the roasting tin holding the water. Bake for
about 1 hour. Let the mould cool to room temperature then
place it in the fridge, preferably overnight (at least six hours).
Place a plate over the mould and turn it over: the flan should
slide out easily. If not, give the mould a firm, careful shake.
Spoon the caramel sauce on top and serve.**

Up close: saving the rainforest

The Amazon rainforest in danger

Tropical rainforests are important to all life on the Earth, but they are being destroyed at an alarming rate.

Logging is a big problem in the Amazon rainforest. Scientists think that about 10 per cent of the trees in the Amazon rainforest have already been cut down by logging companies. These companies look for valuable types of wood found only in the rainforest. If left alone, the trees in these areas may grow again on their own.

After the logging companies cut down all the trees in one area, poor farmers take over. They burn the remaining plants and shrubs to clear the land for planting. This is called 'slash and burn' agriculture. With none of its natural trees, plants and animals, the soil loses its **nutrients**. After only a couple of years, the farmers can no longer use the soil to grow crops. They sell the land to **ranchers** or owners of large plantations.

Ranchers use the land to graze cattle. Plantation owners use it to grow large-scale crops. When nothing more can be done with it, the land is abandoned. Unless conservationists help to regenerate it, the rainforest land becomes useless.

The worst part of this cycle is that it is happening in more than one part of the rainforest. More and more of the rainforest is being destroyed forever, every day.

YELLOW-FACED PARROT ▶
Amazon parrots come in many colours and sizes. Beautiful birds like this are threatened by destruction of the rainforests where they live.

▼ **SLASH AND BURN**
Farmers slash through the plants and then burn the land. This makes it ready for planting crops.

◀ FOREST ON FIRE
Here, trees are burnt to make way for cattle ranching. Ranchers burn many trees at a time.

▲ TREE GRAVEYARD
Cattle are grazed on land cleared of rainforest by ranchers. If new seeds are not planted, the rainforest cannot regrow. It is gone forever.

What is being done to help?

Scientists believe that many species of rainforest animal and plant are becoming **extinct** every day. However, at the same time, people are trying to help the Amazon rainforest and the other rainforests of the world.

Organizations from all over the world work on rainforest **conservation**. The best way to protect the rainforests is to turn large portions of them into **national parks** and **reserves**.

Protected areas are very important for rainforest wildlife. The areas chosen for protection have many different species of animal, bird and insect. They also have species that can survive only in that particular part of the world. Over the last 20 years, the number of national parks in rainforests has grown. Today, almost 5 per cent are protected this way. However, there is still much more work to be done to protect the rainforests and the animals and plants that live in them.

How can you help? You can start by not buying products that cause the destruction of the rainforests. You can help at school by educating your friends about the importance of rainforests. You can join people around the world who care about the rainforests, and become a member of an organization that works to save them. If you join an organization, you'll see that there are many people who care about the rainforests and who are trying to protect them. You can be one of the people who help the rainforests.

Holidays

There are many different national and religious holidays celebrated in Brazil. Brazilians celebrate traditional Christian holidays such as Christmas and Easter. Many cities also honour their patron saints. A patron saint is a saint regarded as the protector of a particular group of people or a country.

The most important public holiday in Brazil is Independence Day. It is on 7 September.

Tiradentes's Day is on 21 April. Tiradentes's real name was Joaquim José da Silva Xavier and he was a revolutionary hero.

Brazil's best-known holiday is Carnival. It is celebrated throughout the country but the celebration in the city of Rio de Janeiro is the most famous. It lasts for five days in February. There are parades, floats, music, people in costumes and dancing. It is lots of fun.

▲ CARNIVAL PARADE
Put on a bright colour and get ready to celebrate. During Carnival, there are parades, music and dancing everywhere.

Learning the language

English	Portuguese	How to say it
Hello	Olá	OH-lah
Good day	Bon dia	bohn DEE-ah
Goodbye	Tchau	CHOW
My name is ___	Meu nome___	MEH-oo NOH-meh
What's your name?	Como é seu nome	KO-mo EH SHE-oo NOH-meh
See you later	Até logo	AH-tay LOW-go
Do you speak English?	Fala inglês	FAH-la in-GLAYSH

Quick facts

Brazil

Capital
Brasilia

Borders
Argentina, Bolivia,
Colombia, French Guiana,
Guyana, Paraguay,
Peru, Suriname, Uruguay
and Venezuela

Area
8,511,965 sq km
(3,286,474 sq miles)

Population
176,029,560

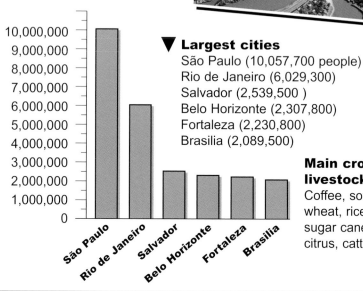

▼ **Largest cities**
São Paulo (10,057,700 people)
Rio de Janeiro (6,029,300)
Salvador (2,539,500)
Belo Horizonte (2,307,800)
Fortaleza (2,230,800)
Brasilia (2,089,500)

**Main crops and
livestock**
Coffee, soya beans,
wheat, rice, maize,
sugar cane, cocoa,
citrus, cattle

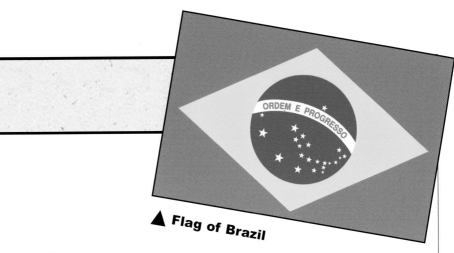

▲ Flag of Brazil

Coastline
7491 km (4654 miles)

Longest river ▶
Amazon
6276 km (3900 miles)

Literacy rate
83% of all Brazilians
can read

Major industries
Textiles, shoes, chemicals,
cement, lumber, iron ore,
tin, steel, aircraft, motor
vehicles and parts,
other machinery
and equipment

Natural resources
Bauxite, gold, iron ore,
manganese, nickel,
phosphates, platinum, tin,
uranium, petroleum,
hydro-power, timber

◀ **Monetary unit**
Reàl

People to know

Many people have made Brazil the fascinating place that it is. Here are a few to find out more about.

◀ Pelé

Pelé's real name is Edson Arantes do Nascimento. You might have heard of him if you like football. At the height of his career, he was the most famous sports personality in the world. He won the World Cup three times with the Brazilian national team.

Sonia Braga ▶

Sonia Braga started her acting career at the age of 14. She is one of Brazil's top actresses. One of her most famous roles was in the 1985 American film *Kiss of the Spider Woman*. Sonia Braga has performed in films and television programmes both in Brazil and the USA.

◀ Antonio Jobim

Antonio Carlos Jobim was one of the founders of the bossa nova movement in music. He was born in 1927 and died in 1994. Jobim composed many famous songs, including *The Girl from Ipanema*.

Do you want to know more about Brazil? Take a look at the books below.

Nations of the World: Brazil,
(Raintree, 2003)
Find out all about Brazil and its people. Learn what it's really like to live there.

Continents: South America, M Fox
(Heinemann Library, 2002)
Learn about the weather, languages, animals, plants, cities, countryside and famous places in Brazil and other countries in South America.

Amazing Journeys: Up a Rainforest Tree,
Rod Theodorou; C Telford
(Heinemann Library, 1998)
Learn about all the plants and animals that live in the Amazon rainforest.

Glossary

abolish put an official end to something

bay wide opening in the shoreline, where the sea is
fairly calm

colony territory settled in or ruled by people from a
state abroad or overseas

conservation protection of nature or wildlife

culture way of life and values of a particular society
or civilization

democracy type of government in which the people
vote for their officials

ecology scientific study of plants and animals in
relation to their surroundings

economy the way a country runs its industry,
trade and money

equator imaginary line around the middle of the
Earth, halfway between the North and South poles

extinct no longer in existence; all members of a group
have died out

humid damp and moist

jury group of people who judge an event

logging cutting down many trees at a time

national park protected area owned by the nation

native belonging by birth or origin to a place

natural resource property of the land, such as water,
plants, wildlife or minerals that occurs naturally and
can be used by humans

nutrient part of the soil that causes things to grow

plantation large farm that grows crops, where the workers live on the land

port place where boats can safely dock to load and unload cargo

prey animal that is hunted for food by another animal

ranch place where cattle or other animals are reared for selling

republic form of government, without a monarch, in which the people vote for their leaders

reserve place such as parkland that is kept in its original state

revolt when people rise in opposition to something

samba Brazilian dance

sea level the average level of the ocean's surface, used for measuring the height or depth of another place

species group of animals or plants that have similar traits and can produce fertile offspring

textile cloth or fabric that has been woven or knitted

timber wood that has been cut for people's use

trade route the path across land or sea taken by traders from many countries so they can buy things from each other.

tropical climate that is hot with heavy rainfall

Index